Let's Play Tag!

Read the Page

Say It   Sound It   Spell It

Why is wh yellow?

Yellow highlights represent letter teams
that make a single sound or words
with irregular decoding patterns.

INTERNET CONNECTION REQUIRED FOR AUDIO DOWNLOAD.
To use this book with the Tag™ Reader you must download audio from the LeapFrog® Connect Application.
The LeapFrog Connect Application can be downloaded and installed at leapfrog.com/connect.

Leap's Snack

Story by Suzanne Barchers
Illustrated by Yakovetic Productions

 Leap and Dan have fun digging in the sand.

They plan a castle.
Tad lends a hand.

Tad wants a snack. He acts like a grump and starts to fuss.

"Don't worry, Tad.
Let's go back and fix
a grand snack for all
of us," Leap says.

"What will I fix? I have a plan."

Leap grabs his stuff and gets a big pan.

 "You can fix fruit," says Dan. "We can eat plums."

"You can fix ham
and melted cheese
on a bun. Yum-yum!"
says Tad.

 "I know!" Leap
says as he gives Tad
a wink.

Leap mixes and
stirs. Then he stops
for a drink.

 "What did he fix?"

"What went in the mix?"

13

Leap brings the snack out in a sack.

Tad looks in the
sack and his lips go
smack, smack!

 Tad says, "Thanks Leap! What a great snack!"

Words You're Learning
Consonant Blends and CK Pattern

Final Blends

acts	grump	sand
and	hand	went
drink	lends	wink
grand	melted	

ck Pattern

back
sack
smack
snack

Sight Words

do	off	what
for	the	you
look	to	

Challenging Words

brings	fruit	like	stirs
castle	gives	looks	thanks
cheese	great	need	then
digging	know	out	we
don't	let's	starts	worry
eat			